GET CRAFTY

INDOOR CRAFTS

Vivienne Bolton

DP

DEMPSEY
PARR

Editor
Barbara Segall

Art Direction
Full Steam Ahead

DesignTeam
Design Study

Photography
Patrick Spillane

Photographic Co-ordinator
Liz Spillane

Styling
Bianca Boulton

Project Management
Kate Miles

The publishers would like to thank Inscribe Ltd., Bordon, Hants. for
providing the art materials used in these projects and
Sophie Boulton for her assistance.

First published in 1998 by
Dempsey Parr
Queen Street House, 4–5 Queen Street, Bath
BA1 1HE

24681097531

Copyright © Dempsey Parr 1998

Produced by Miles Kelly Publishing Ltd
Unit 11, Bardfield Centre, Great Bardfield, Essex CM7 4SL

British Library Cataloguing-in-Publication Data
A catalogue record for this book is available from the British Library.

ISBN 1-84084-399-3

Printed in Italy

INDOOR CRAFTS

Contents

Bookmarks

Bookmarks will always come in handy, whether you enjoy fairy tales or mysteries. These bookmarks are made from thin cardboard and colored with felt-tip pens. A bookmark made from your initial written in bubble writing and decorated with bright colors would take no time to make. You could take inspiration from the book you are reading or make one representing a particular hobby or interest.

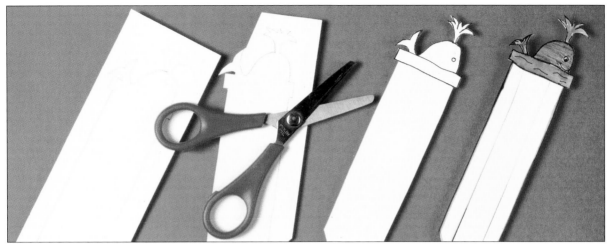

1 Use pencil to outline the whale. When you are happy with the shape cut it out.

Use felt-tip pens to color in the design and draw a neat border with a black felt-tip pen.

2 Personalize your bookmark by using your initial. Draw the outline in pencil first,

then go over it with a felt-tip pen before you decorate the inner part of the initial.

3 This bookmark would look good in a gardening book!

You will need:
Thin cardboard
Pencil
Scissors
Felt-tip pens

Paper Flowers

S urprise a friend with a bunch of scarlet poppies and fantasy flowers. They are made from tissue paper and florist's wire. The poppies are made up of individual petals and look quite realistic with their black-fringed stamens. The fantasy flowers are easy to make from layers of different colors. Let your imagination run riot and create a rainbow bouquet.

You will need:

Glue

Tissue paper in a variety of colors

Florist's wire

Green florist's tape

Scissors

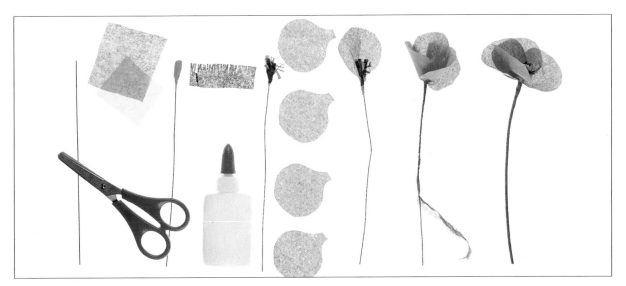

1 Glue a scrunched-up piece of tissue paper onto one end of a piece of wire, for the center of the poppy. Now glue the square of green paper over the poppy center. Roll the black-fringed piece around the center of the flower to make the stamens. Glue on the petals one at a time. Bend them slightly so they look realistic. Finally, use the green tape to tidy up the base of the flower and cover the wire.

2 Fantasy flowers are made from layers of colored flower shapes. Begin by cutting the shape for the base or sepals of the flower. Layer three colors of tissue paper together, cut out a flower shape, and then cut a small hole through the center of the papers. Wind a small piece of paper around a wire to make the flower center. Now use glue to attach the green sepal shape and the colored flowers. Finally use the green tape to tidy up the base of the flower and cover the wire.

Making paper flowers takes practice. Don't expect the first one to come out perfectly. Keep trying until you get a good shape make a bunch.

Teddy Bears

Make a whole family of cut-out bears and design outfits for them—playclothes, fancy dress, pajamas. These bears are drawn on thin, white cardboard and colored with pencil crayons. If you do not have any cardboard to hand, use cardboard from a cereal box to make the bears and their outfits. A simple folded bed would be fun to decorate.

You will need:

Thin cardboard or stiff paper

Pencil

Crayons

Scissors

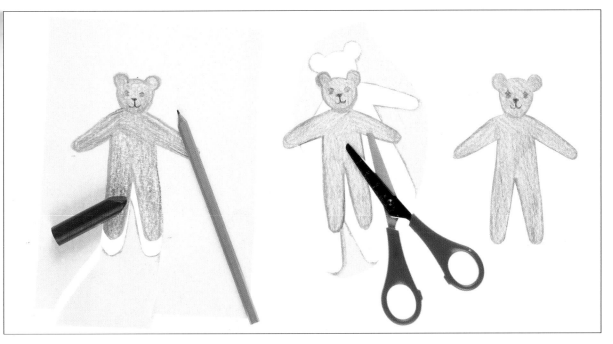

1 Draw a teddy bear onto thin cardboard. Give it a face and color it in using bright crayon colors. Cut it out. Make several members of a teddy bear family to dress.

2 Lay the cut-out teddy bears onto paper or thin cardboard and draw an outfit around each shape. Fill in and color.

Remember to tidy away all the scraps of paper and cardboard when you have made your cut-out bears.

FELT
Beads

Turn ethnic-looking beads made from colored felt into great chokers, bracelets, and pendants. The beads are made from layers of felt glued or tied together. They are threaded on embroidery silk. Make a selection of colors and shapes and combine them with wooden beads to make an exotic necklace.

You will need:

Felt squares (from a craft shop)

Scissors

Fabric glue

Rubber band

Needle and colored thread

Small quantity of stuffing

Ribbon

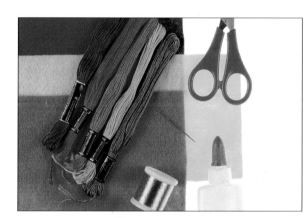

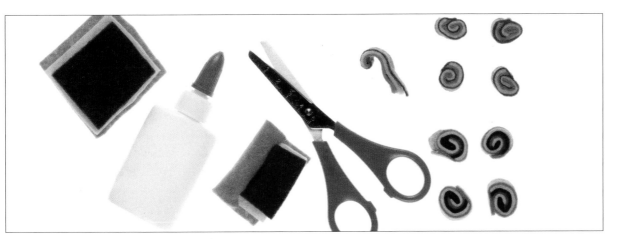

1 Cut three squares of colored felt, each slightly smaller than the other. Layer them, using a little glue to hold them in place. Now roll them tightly in a sausage shape and hold in place with glue. You may need to wind a little thread around them or hold them in place with a rubber band. The glue will need to dry thoroughly. When the glue has set, use scissors to cut the sausage into beads.

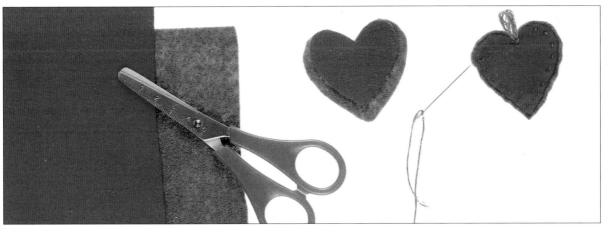

2 You will need two squares of colored felt. Cut out a heart shape from each color, with one heart slightly smaller than the other. Place a little stuffing between the layers and sew them together with colored thread. Make a ribbon loop at the top of the heart for threading.

3 Roll up a small square of felt. Hold the roll in place with glue. Wind colored thread around the sausage-shaped felt pieces to make decorative bands.

Friendship Bracelets

Friendship bracelets are easier to make than you think; they just take a little time to practice. Choose several threads in strong or pastel color combinations. Find a corner to settle down on your own where you can work without interruption and in time you will master the art and make a braid to wear and one to give to a special friend.

You will need:

Cork board or work surface

Selection of colored thread

Sticky tape or safety pins

Scissors

1 You will need three lengths of thread. Make a knot to hold the threads together and attach the knot end to the board or work surface with tape or a safety pin.

5 To start row two, make knots from left to right; knot B twice onto C, then twice onto A. For the third row, knot C twice onto A, then twice onto B.

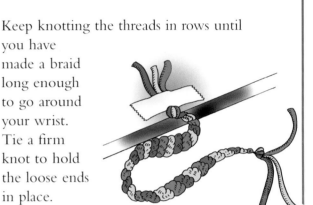

2 Hold thread B with your left hand; Take thread A around B and push it through the loop to make a knot and pull the thread.

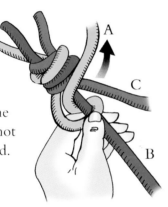

6 Keep knotting the threads in rows until you have made a braid long enough to go around your wrist. Tie a firm knot to hold the loose ends in place.

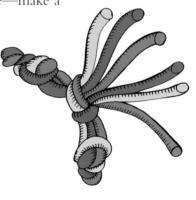

3 Repeat this action. You should have two knots on thread B.

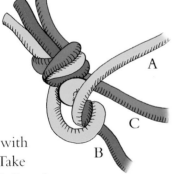

7 Your friendship bracelet is now complete—make a double knot at each end and trim away any excess thread.

4 Hold thread C with your left hand. Take thread A around C and through the loop to make a knot. Pull the thread and then do it again. You should now have two knots on thread C. Thread A is now on the righthand side and you have completed the first row.

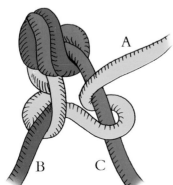

Remember to protect your work surface with newspaper or a vinyl cloth.

To make a wider braid use four, five, or six threads. Make the braid as described above, knotting each thread twice, from left to right.

Brooches

Use oven-bake clay to make these cheeky brooches. Glitter-spangled stars, leaping dolphins, tiny toadstools, or a fat pink pig—these will all look great on a felt beret or a coat lapel. The glitter star is made from colored clay with the glitter glued on after baking. A coat of varnish gives a good finish.

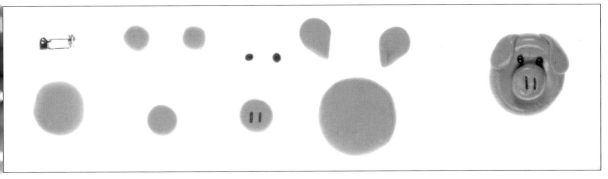

1 To make this pink pig brooch start with a disk of pink clay to make the face. The nose is made from a small cylinder shape. Use the modeling tool or a cocktail stick to mark nostrils on the nose. The ears are made from flattened tear drop shapes flapping over the face. Make two little black eyes and when all the parts are assembled, place your pig brooch on an oven tray, ready for baking.

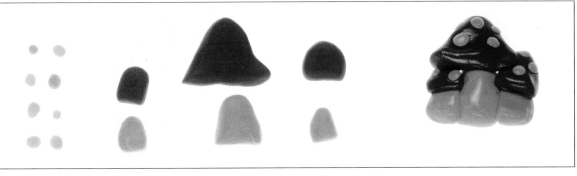

2 To make a cluster of toadstools, begin by making three stalks, one large and two small, out of yellow clay. Squash them gently together. Now make the caps from red clay and press them carefully onto the stalks. Decorate the caps with tiny yellow dots and your toadstool brooch is now ready for baking. After baking, when the clay has cooled, varnish the shapes. With an adult's help, glue on the brooch backs.

You will need:

Oven-bake clay in a variety of colors

Modeling tool

Oven tray

Varnish

Brooch backs

Suitable glue

When using oven-bake clay you will need to soften the clay first by molding it between your fingers.

Follow the manufacturer's directions when baking the clay.

Always have an adult present when using the oven.

Ask an adult for help when attaching the fastener to the brooch as you will need to use a strong glue.

Candy Cushions

Dyed with wax crayons, these cushions will look soft and cuddly on your bed or on the playroom sofa. The cushions are made with calico fabric and are easy shapes to cut out and decorate. The wax crayon patterns can be ironed on to set them firmly. You could make a whole bag of candy cushions for your bed. A calico cat or doll would be great fun to decorate with wax crayons.

You will need:

Calico fabric

Wax crayons

Scissors

Needle and thread

Polyester stuffing

Brown paper

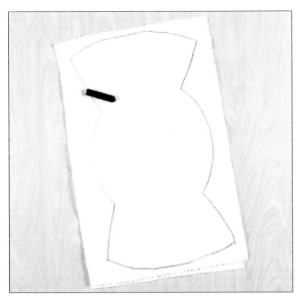

1 Fold the fabric in half to make a double layer. Draw on a large wrapped candy shape on the calico.

3 Cut out the cushion shapes and turn them right sides in. Sew together leaving a gap for the stuffing.

2 Use the wax crayons to color the candy shape in swirls and dots, making it as realistic as possible.

4 Turn right side out. At this stage you should ask an adult to help iron the cushion shape between brown paper to seal the dye. Stuff the cushion with polyester.

RECYCLED PLASTIC
Mobiles

Recycle milk and juice containers and turn them into colorful mobiles. The sleepy sheep would look good above your bed and the stars and flowers could hang in a sunny window. The mobiles are painted using water-soluble glass paints and outliners. If you don't have those to hand you can use colored, permanent markers instead to create a similar effect.

You will need:
Florist's wire
Small pliers
Flat sided plastic milk or drink carton
Scissors
Outliner
Paintbrushes
Water-soluble glass paints
Needle
Gold thread

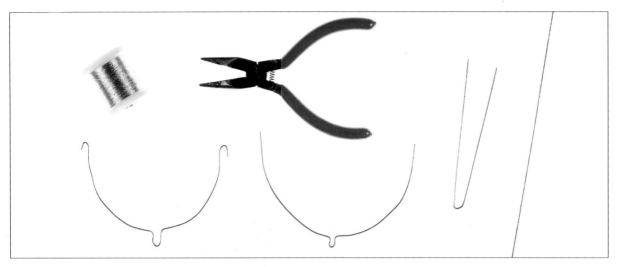

1 Florist's wire is easy to bend; start with an 8 in. length. Begin by folding it in half. Then use the pliers to shape the mobile hanger and hooks. You will need three hangers for each mobile and each hanger should be exactly the same shape and size.

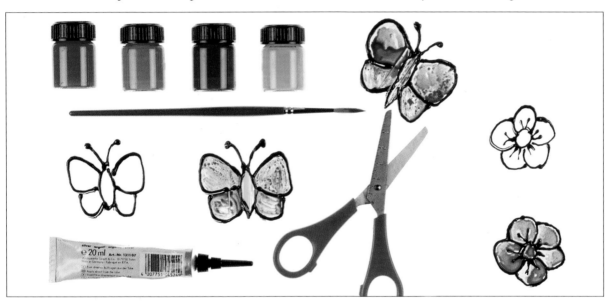

2 Use the scissors to cut the plastic container into suitable shapes for decoration. Wash the shapes and dry with a clean cloth. Outline the design and when the outliner is hard use a dry brush and glass paint to color the shape.

3 Assemble the mobile by making a hole with the needle through the shapes and threading the gold thread through. Hang up the shapes and your mobile is complete.

Letter Rack

Keep your mail in check with these bright red tulips! The letter rack is made by slotting together thick colored card shapes. Once you have mastered the technique you will be able to create your own designs, such as these flower patterns, or maybe have a go at the ship at sea. The ship is a little more detailed, with the design cut from colored paper.

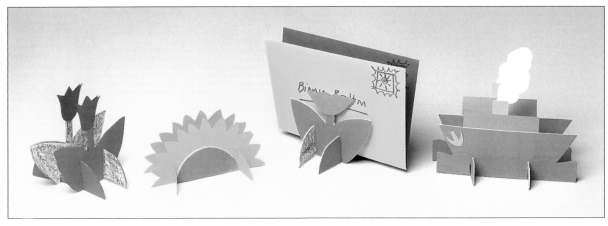

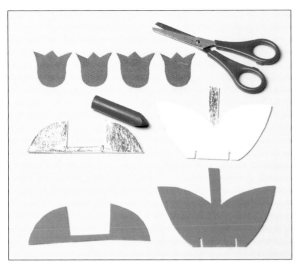

1 Draw the design on thick, colored cardboard. The green bases will need to be cut straight to stand level on the table. The flowerheads are cut from colored paper. Cut all the pieces out.

2 Color the plain side of the card with crayons. Slot the letter rack together. You may need to make a rough one first to get the shape and slots right.

The letter rack can be made of cardboard cut from a cereal or grocery box. You may need to cover the pieces of card with a layer of papier-mâché to make them more sturdy and create a good surface to paint or color.

3 Glue on the flower heads and your letter rack is ready to hold the mail.

You will need:

Thick colored cardboard

Scissors

Colored paper

Crayons

Glue

Thin colored cardboard

Mirror Painting

irror, mirror on the wall who is the fairest of us all? Paint one of these pretty designs on a mirror tile to put up on the bathroom wall. The tiles are painted with glass paint, which is available in a wide selection of colors and is very easy to use. The outliner divides the colors and comes in tubes that you use like a ballpoint pen, squeezing the color gently onto the mirror.

You will need:

Mirror tiles or handbag mirrors

Glass paint outliners

Paper towel to mop up spills

Paintbrushes

Water-soluble glass paints

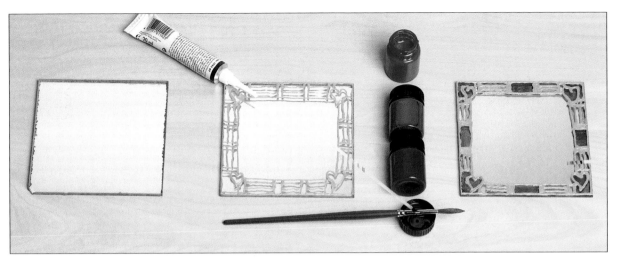

1 Use the outliner as if it were a pen, squeezing gently to allow a steady stream of the thick liquid onto the glass. Keep your paper towels handy in case of spills.

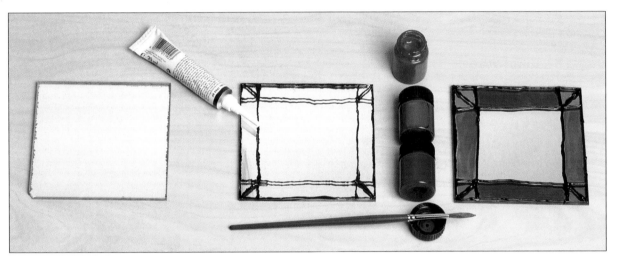

2 When the outliner is completely hard you can paint in the color. Use a dry brush to dip into one color at a time and wash and dry the brush well between colors.

Wirework

Colored furry wire is a great craft material as it is easy to form into flowers, leaves, and other fancy shapes. Fill a small flower pot with wire flowers for a pretty gift, or make a bunch of red blooms to brighten up a dull corner. Glitter wire can be shaped into stars and hearts, and pressed into cork to make a romantic message.

You will need:

Colored furry wire

Glitter wire

Felt-tip pen

1 Bend the red wire into a flower shape. Wind the end of a piece of green wire around the centre of the flower—leave the long end to form the stalk.

Make the leaves by winding green wire around a felt-tip pen then easing it off. It will hold its shape. Put the flowers and leaves into a vase.

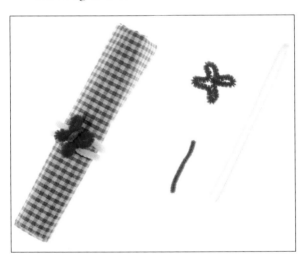

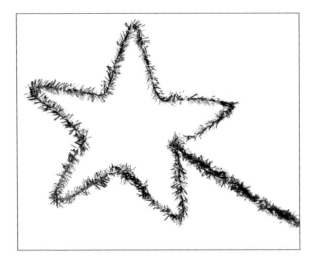

2 To make a napkin holder bend the white wire to form a circle. Decorate with a red wire flower. Fix it on with green wire.

3 Shape silver wires into these attractive table decorations. Push the shaped wire into cork to make a support or stand.

Bent furry wire can be straightened by pulling it between a finger and thumb a number times until it resumes its original shape.

Animal Pegs

Hold notes to your clipboard with a wild animal peg. The animals are drawn, cartoon-style, on thin cardboard and colored using felt-tip pens. You could try gluing one of the finished pegs onto a magnet and attaching it to the fridge to hold notes. Practice your drawing on scrap paper first and look at comic strips and story book illustrations to get the style right.

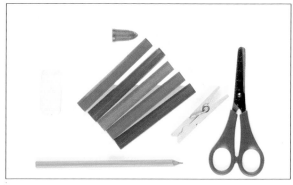

You will need:

Thin cardboard

Pencil

Scissors

Felt-tip pens

Eraser

Glue

Pegs

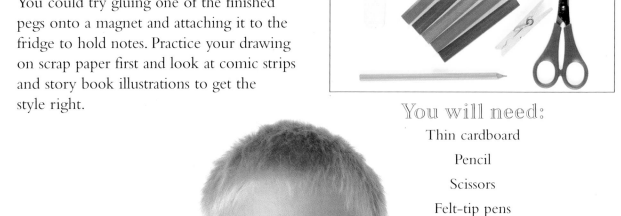

Have a good look at these examples before you begin. Draw an outline with pencil. When you are happy with the shape, color in the animal using felt–tip pens. If you draw a dark outline around the colored animal, you will see that this makes a big difference and gives the picture a professional finish. Cut out your animal and glue it onto a peg.

Miniature Farm

This miniature farm can be made in an afternoon and could provide endless pleasure for a younger brother or sister. Stand it on a sunny windowsill to create a pretty country scene. Make a storage box for the farm from a matchbox covered with coloured paper and decorated in farmyard-style.

You will need:

Oven-bake clay

Modeling tool and cocktail stick

Oven tray

Matchbox

Colored paper

Scissors

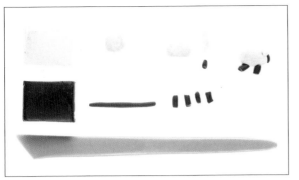

1 Begin by softening the white clay. Make the body first, then flatten a strip and fold it over the body as the ears. Now soften a small piece of black clay, and roll it into a sausage shape. Use the modeling tool to cut the legs and face.

2 These colorful hens are made from a small ball of brown clay. Press the clay to shape the head and tail of the hen. Make a base from a ball of green clay. Pinch out tiny pieces of red and yellow clay for the beak and comb.

3 First soften the pink clay. Make a nice round sausage shape for the body. The pig's snout is made from a small flattened ball and its ears are made from flattened teardrop shapes. Roll out a smaller sausage shape and use the modeling tool to cut short legs. Roll out a thin tail and attach it firmly to the body.

To make some little patches of daisy-covered grass flatten an oval shape of green clay. Then make some small balls of yellow and green clay and use a cocktail stick or the tip of your modeling tool to lift them up and press them down onto the clay grass. When all your models are made, place them on a baking tray and harden them in the oven.

Follow the manufacturer's directions when baking the clay.

If you can't buy oven bake clay, you can use modeling clay.

Scrunchies

Easy to make, you can have a scrunchy for every occasion. Sew them by hand in a running stitch or ask an adult to sew them for you, using a sewing machine. Thread them with elastic and decorate them imaginatively. Make scrunchies from ribbon, lace, velvet, or dress fabric. A brightly colored toweling scrunchy would be good for the seaside or swimming pool.

You will need:

Fabric and lace

Needle and thread or a sewing machine

Medium-sized safety pin

One quarter inch wide elastic

Scissors

Sequins and glue

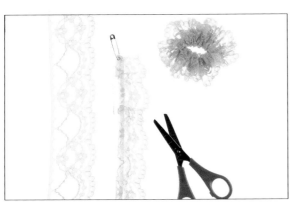

1 Lace: sew a half-inch wide hem along one edge of the lace. Use the safety pin to thread the elastic through the seam. Tie the ends of the elastic into a knot and shape the scrunchy.

3 Tartan: this attractive scrunchy is made in the same way as the velvet scrunchy. Use matching thread to sew the seams.

2 Velvet: fold the fabric in half lengthways, with the wrong side out. Sew a seam. Turn the velvet tube the right way round by pulling one end through the other. Sew a channel in matching thread along one side and thread the elastic through.

4 Sequin: make this party-time scrunchy in the same way as the tartan and velvet scrunchies. Decorate it with shiny sequins glued or sewn onto the fabric.

Index